IN ADVERSITY THERE IS HOPE

An Epic Life Journey

By

ANNA GREAVES

To my children Max, Julia and Maria, to my granddaughter Astrid, to my husband Steve and to my 'adopted' son Russell

CONTENTS

CHAPTER 1

MY HUMBLE BEGINNINGS

My earliest memory is of an unpleasant episode that happened when I was very young. If I am not mistaken, we normally remember things from around the age of three, but this vivid and indelible scene occurred when I was only about two years old.

The setting was a room hardly furnished, with an old chest alongside one of the walls and only a few chairs scattered here and there. There were numerous people sleeping on the floor in this very dark room - dark because it must have been the middle of the night. I don't know who those people were. Those lying on the floor on makeshift beds must have been my brothers and sisters. I don't remember my parents being there, though my mother at least must have been nearby. The moonlight flickered through the small window which had neither curtains nor shutters. In the distance, you could hear the noise of aircraft flying low in the sky; there must have been an air raid happening that night.

My father was often away working as a bricklayer, even then, when the war was still in full swing. In fact, he used to have to travel to a town further south called Foggia to work. He came back for a couple of days once a month or so. Foggia was quite a distance away - about 100 miles. It is unbelievable to think that he cycled there and back each time!

In one corner of the room at least two people were sleeping on chairs: one was my beloved paternal grandmother, Maria Vincenza, a generous and unselfish woman who showered us with much love and affection. I remember her very fondly. She died in 1968, a few weeks after she heard that I had given birth to a son; she was delighted by the news. The remarkable thing was that, aged seventy, her hair was still black! (Luckily, I seem to have inherited that trait). Sadly, I had not seen her for two years when she passed away, which was a shame. When I heard that she had died, I cried non-stop for two whole days, as I was totally devastated and missed her so much. I still miss her now! What an amazing person she was!

On the other chair was her partner, Don Cesare,

who was much older than she was. He was educated and highly respected as a land surveyor in this poor corner of the Abruzzi region. This is not an area too well known to the British, who seem to prefer other regions such as Tuscany and Umbria; the latter is adjacent to Abruzzi. However, this section of central Italy is of a breath-taking beauty, with a dramatic landscape and, in the interior, there are hills with ancient villages sitting on them and also the Appennines, the backbone of Italy.

The two highest peaks of this mountain range are amazing. The higher one of the two is called 'Gran Sasso'. Gabriele D'Annunzio, the poet born in Pescara (he was the leading writer in Italy in the late 19th and the early 20th centuries), referred to it as the 'Bella

Addormentata' (The Sleeping Beauty) because, with a little imagination, looking at its outline it is possible to visualize the head and the bosom of a woman. Gran Sasso, which has a small glacier, can be clearly seen from Chieti (the city where I was born) and from the windows of the flat belonging to my family, providing a spectacular sight when the sun sets behind it. The other peak, even closer to Chieti than Gran Sasso, is called 'La Maiella'. The sun rises behind the latter, which also looks stunning especially in the morning. In the interior there is also a National Park, with brown bears and wolves. Altogether it is a region of immeasurable rugged beauty. It is an ideal place to go skiing on the pistes of the Appennines in winter and in summer to sunbathe on golden sandy beaches, which look out onto the emerald waters of the Adriatic Sea.

After Don Cesare met my grandmother, despite her illiteracy and the fact that she had three small children under the age of five, he proposed an arrangement that she could not refuse, i.e. that they should live together instead of getting married, so that she would not lose her war widow's pension. Furthermore, he made her realize that, if she agreed to move in with him, her children would have a substitute father, a male figure to look up to. My grandfather had been killed in the First World War in battle and had left her widowed with three children under the age of five. She was devastated by his premature demise and literally went mad. Thankfully, she recovered and made the decision to be 'in lutto', that is to wear only black clothes for the rest of her life in remembrance of her dead husband. That she did!

As Don Cesare had offered her a comfortable standard of living and had promised to take care of her children, after much soul searching, she agreed to 'live in sin' with him, as bigots used to describe the liaison. Tongues wagged and people criticized and condemned her, but she gritted her teeth and moved in with him. It was typical of her to sacrifice herself for others, especially her beloved children, two boys and a girl. Later on in her life, she used to spend hours and hours in church, begging God to forgive her for what she believed was the terrible sin of not marrying the man she lived with until his death. I am not sure when he died, but it couldn't have been long after the end of the Second World War, as he was not around when I was five years old and I have no further memories of him after the original incident I am describing below.

Going back to that dark room, I remember waking up, sitting up and looking towards the two chairs, as I saw a movement from Don Cesare. What I witnessed next suddenly reappeared in my memory years later, having laid dormant in the deepest recesses of my brain. When I realized the significance of that extraordinary scene, I felt utter revulsion and anger at the thought of me, at the time a poor innocent little girl, just a toddler, suddenly thrust into a sordid adult world. He had exposed himself to me! What made this even more horrible was his gesture, which invited me to go to him, as his lips made a quiet sound "Vieni qui. Vieni qui" (Come here. Come here). In my innocence I must have realized that there was something nasty about all that, because I remember being very frightened and lying down again. Years later, when I remembered what he had done, although it all seems mild in comparison to the horror stories we hear nowadays about paedophiles, I thought, "The wretched man! What a despicable thing to do!" I don't know why I kept this secret and only told my elder sister when I was in my early thirties, as if I had felt a sense of guilt about the whole incident.

I was born Anna Di Lorenzo in the spring of 1942, on Friday the 13th, whilst the Second World War raged around my family and my place of birth, Chieti, which eventually was declared 'Citta`Aperta' (Open City) by the Allies in 1944. Chieti is a very ancient, historical city, apparently even older than Rome. It used to be called Teate, in honour of the goddess Teti. It sits proudly on a hill, like most villages and towns in

Abruzzo and is one of the four major cities in the region; its views all round are amazing.

Well, as we said, it was agreed by the Allies that Chieti should be preserved, so it became an Open City. Unfortunately, the Germans took advantage of this fact and quickly settled there. They only left the day before the Allies liberated it on the 9th June 1944. They clearly wanted to make the most of the fact that there would be no more bombings in that city. Interestingly, the battles of the Sangro and Moro rivers at the end of 1943 were not too far from Chieti, close to a town called Ortona. Sadly, many British and Canadian soldiers were killed in the fierce fighting which went on for days and now rest in two large military cemeteries.

The fifth of six children, I was apparently only

conceived so that my father would not continue fighting in the war (my brother Franco followed a year or so later for the very same reason!), with the possibility that he might be killed like his own father. Indeed, my paternal grandfather, Domenico Di Lorenzo, died a hero in the First World War, at the age of just twenty-five. He had only been at the front for a few weeks when he was sent to the virtual slaughter which took place on the Isonzo river in the north of Italy, where battles ensued between the Austro-Hungarian and Italian armies from June 1915 to November 1917.

My paternal grandparents had not spent much of their married life together, as my grandfather, due to the great poverty which afflicted rural Italy at the time, had gone to do seasonal work in Canada and only returned when called up to serve his Country. We have recently found the records of the ship which took him to Canada. I wish he had stayed there, instead of returning just to be killed.

The death of my grandfather had long-term repercussions for my father and ultimately for me too. After the First World War the Italian Government, in its meagre generosity, decided that only one of his three very young children left without a father should be given a grant for free education and free boarding.

Education in Italy at the time, although officially compulsory, was not well funded by the State, therefore it was too expensive for most families. Children only went to school for two or three years, with huge sacrifices on the part of their parents, and then left to learn a trade. My grandmother was faced with a big dilemma, as she had to choose which one of her three children should be given the better start in life that only education can ensure for those who receive it.

Her partner, Don Cesare, as we know, had had a good education and was very clever, so my grandmother had complete trust in his wisdom. His advice was that my aunt Grazia should be given the opportunity to study, as a substitute for the dowry that her mother was unable to give her. The two boys - my father and his younger brother - would learn a trade, so they would be able to support themselves and their families. My aunt was sent to boarding school until she became a primary school teacher, my father learnt bricklaying after a small stint with a cobbler and my uncle Domenico acquired the skills of a locksmith.

Unfortunately, my aunt taught for only two years after qualifying as a primary school teacher, then got married and never went back into teaching. What a waste! Of course, her children benefited, as she was able to guide them through their own schooling, unlike me and my brothers who had to fend for ourselves, with the result that my childhood was very poor, deprived and neglected, to be honest. Also, we never had any help with our homework, as my father was rarely there and my mother was not up to it, although she was quite clever too. Not surprisingly, my brothers never went too far with their studies because they had nobody to guide them in the constant absence of my father.

At first, we lived in poverty and squalor. Not the best

of starts in life! There were no safety nets such as the 'dole' or 'benefits' in Italy at the time. I believe that even now there is not really a great network to support poor people over there. It is probably because extended families rally around to give help, whilst in the UK support is provided mainly by the State and charitable organisations.

My father worked very hard to try to provide for his large brood, but money was scarce and often he couldn't even find a job, as poverty was widespread in Italy and there was little or no money for building work. Also, food shortages were rife in general and in Abruzzo in particular.

My parents had eloped at a relatively young age. My father was twenty-three and my mother was twenty.

My maternal grandfather had opposed the relationship, as my father was deemed to be socially beneath my mother's family, which apparently, they believed, had blue blood in it. Ironically, recently I discovered that my father's family origins are much more sound, as I have been able to trace my forebears on that side up to the beginning of the 18th century and established that they were relatively wealthy. Indeed, in the 19th century my father's ancestors were landowners, but it was traditional to divide the land equally amongst all the sons and daughters, so their wealth was diluted with every generation. The last small pieces of land were inherited by my grandmother and her three brothers, two of whom lived in Pianella, about twenty km from Chieti, and looked after their smallholding which provided a subsistence standard of living.

I remember visiting them with my grandmother when I was about twelve. They were harvesting their meagre wheat crop by hand, using sickles, as there was no machinery available then. I will never forget the torrid heat which was typical of June at that time when the seasons were well-defined, and the wheat, dotted with innumerable red poppies, swaying in the stifling breeze.

As far as sickles are concerned, many accidents resulted from their usage. In fact, my uncle Domenico one day injured his left eye whilst collecting grass for his rabbits on a roadside verge. He had strayed onto the road and, when a car appeared suddenly, he tried to get away by grabbing the sack full of grass with the hand holding the sickle. His gauche and hurried movement meant that the tip of the sickle landed in his left eye, which he lost as a result. Some years later, as it was difficult to source glass eyes in Italy, I had to buy them for him in the UK.

There is certainly no blue blood in my mother's family, which actually stems from an unmarried mother on one side and an orphan on the other. However, on a positive note, I have discovered that one of my mother's ancestors who lived in the 19th century was in fact a surgeon and several others were quite literate, which was unusual in those days in Italy. Furthermore, several ancestors were also described as landowners and 'wealthy'; unfortunately, all the wealth had dissipated by the time my mother was born. My great-great maternal grandmother was a Capone, although not at all connected to the Mafia, I am sure! Also, many of my mother's female ancestors lived to a ripe old age of 90 and above, which was not common in the 19th century.

Apparently, there were many illicit relationships even in those days and any child born out of wedlock was abandoned in 'the wheel', an arrangement which allowed the mother to remain anonymous. Orphanages had holes in the wall containing some sort of container, which could be rotated after a baby was furtively placed in it. That is what happened to my maternal great-grandfather: he had in fact been left in a 'wheel'. He was also doubly unlucky, as he lived a very short life and died at around forty years of age.

Although I am not sure of the dates - I cannot ask

any senior members of my family, as they have all passed away now - we lived on the top floor of a house on the outskirts of Chieti. The three-storey building belonged to the family of my uncle Domenico's wife, who kindly had given us hospitality in those difficult times. Every night before dark we had to go into the shelter, which was really just a large and deep hole carved by my father and my uncle out of the side of the hill that flanked our dwelling. One night, when I was about three months old, I was unwell and feverish with a bad cough, so my mother wanted me and her to stay in the house instead of going into the shelter with the rest of the family. My father insisted that it was safer if we joined the rest of the family, so my mother agreed very reluctantly to do just that. Well, that night a bomb was dropped on the house! The cot in which I would have slept was apparently blown to smithereens! My father and my uncle tried to patch up the damage to the building and indeed we continued to live there, still using the shelter every night. However, for a while, we had to share my uncle's flat on the ground floor, or what remained of it, with him and his wife. It must have been very crowded, as each floor of the house was not vast.

Sometime after the bombing of the house, an incident happened which made my parents think that enough was enough and it was time to move to the countryside, away from the city and the German soldiers who used to walk into houses looking for women to rape. Indeed, one day they arrived at our house. However, when some of the soldiers walked into the bedroom, they saw my mother in bed, having very recently given birth to my youngest brother; the other five of us were sitting on the bed. The German soldiers thankfully took pity on us all and decided to leave my mother alone.

Continuing to live in Chieti also put my father in grave danger, as apparently the Germans had a habit of retaliating if the resistance sabotaged any of their equipment; this happened regularly. The Nazi soldiers would round up all the younger men in a village or zone of the city deemed to be the source of the problem, march them to a waste ground outside the city, order them to dig a grave and then shoot them, so their bodies would fall in.

One day my parents gathered their few possessions, including a wardrobe which was left with a hole in its door caused by shrapnel when the bomb fell on the house. They put the six children, all under the age of seven, in the wardrobe after removing its door and placed it on a large cart - presumably they tied it to the cart, to ensure it did not slip off! Then my mother pushed and my father pulled the rudimentary means of transport all the way to the village where my grandmother's family lived: Pianella. The distance they had to cover on foot was about twenty kilometres. My grandmother helped as best as she could; Don Cesare just struggled behind with his walking stick. The wardrobe is still in the family and still displays the shrapnel-damaged door.

The scene I described earlier must have happened sometime between my brother Franco's birth in

September 1943 and the departure of the Germans from Abruzzi in June 1944. We stayed in Pianella for a few years after the war ended, mainly because we could at least continue to live on the smallholding belonging to my paternal grandmother Maria Vincenza's brothers.

I have only two other memories of this period of my life. The first one is of two plum trees outside the house we stayed in: they bore very dark plums, which I thought were absolutely delicious. Their leaves were of a reddish purple and the colour of the fruit almost matched the foliage.

The second memory is of when one of my brothers, Domenico, injured his foot so badly that I remember blood gushing out and colouring the soil bright red.

Someone came to the rescue and plunged his foot into a bowl of water. I don't remember what happened next. I just know that we had been running, with no shoes on as usual, over the freshly ploughed fields around the house we stayed in; unfortunately, metal shards from the recent bombings - which the ploughing had unearthed - were everywhere, so running around barefoot was quite hazardous.

When I was thirteen years old, I stayed a few weeks with some people we knew in Orsogna, another village in Abruzzo. Their teenage children took me along with them when they went to scour the recently turned-over earth to collect as many pieces of metal as we could find, to sell and get some pocket money: that was the first money I ever earned and it felt amazing. There was so much metal in those fields that we were struggling under the weight of kilos of it after barely a couple of hours of searching.

CHAPTER 2

AFTER THE WAR ENDED

When the war was thankfully over in 1945, my father wanted to go back to Chieti where he could find work more easily. However, he had nowhere for his family to stay, least of all with my maternal grandparents who lived in a very small house on the outskirts of the city and therefore had no room for eight more people. There were very few blocks of flats being built in and around Chieti, so it was difficult to find accommodation. Money was also scarce because, whatever he earned, was hardly sufficient to feed his family. Having little money made my mother always moody and miserable, something I hated throughout my childhood.

My father devised a cunning plan. He was working in Chieti, building five four-storey blocks of council flats, which were quite affordable, but had unfortunately already been reserved for others. When the first one was almost complete and just about habitable, he took us all back to Chieti from Pianella and installed us in one of the two flats on the top floor. The Council officials could not really evict six young children with nowhere to go, so eventually they allowed us to stay. The flat is still in the family, as my parents bought it outright several decades later. It was a very robust building, with very thick walls which would have been ideal in the event of an earthquake; in fact, my father often said that, if there was a tremor, we should go and stand in the doorways of the flat because they were so wide that they would not collapse. A balcony was added decades later, but it wasn't there whilst I was growing up.

The danger of earthquakes is unfortunately very real in most of Italy, especially along the Appennines. In fact, there was a very serious earthquake only a few years ago near Gran Sasso, in a city called L'Aquila. My friend's daughter, her unborn child, her three-year-old little boy and her husband, all perished when their house collapsed. More than three hundred other people also died. A terrible tragedy! How do you ever recover from something like that? I really feel for my poor friend, as it must have been so hard to come to terms with such a tragic loss. I too cannot forget those lovely people who lost their lives in such a terrible way.

So, we finally had a home! I was five years old when we moved in. The flat was rather small, with one large bedroom which we called 'La Siberia'. There were two smaller bedrooms, one tiny bathroom with no bath or shower at the time (a bath was added later) and one medium dining room adjacent to a very small kitchen. We had no heating, so the flat was very cold in winter.

Except for my parents who had their own bedroom, 'La Siberia' was where we all slept. We had to sleep two to each bed, head-to-toe. It was so uncomfortable, especially when we became teenagers, as there wasn't really room for two of us in one small bed. I had to share with my sister Rita; I don't know how, but I often found myself on the floor in the morning! Did she push me off the bed in the night? I always wondered. That did not help the way we felt about each other, as in those days we did not seem to have much in common; our relationship improved when we became adults though. Sleeping in the Siberia room was really like sleeping in a fridge! The rest of the flat was not much warmer. I remember, later on, when I was about fourteen years old, visiting a school friend at home in winter. I was amazed at how warm it was in that flat! I even admired the ceramic water receptacles placed on the radiators to keep the air moist. It was truly a case of finding out how the other half lived.

At some point, years after we moved in, a small coal-fire stove was placed in the very small kitchen so we could sit around it, but there wasn't room for everyone. Luckily the local bakery sold hot ashes, which my grandmother Maria Vincenza would purchase every day in winter. I cannot remember how she brought them home, but they must have been carried in some sort of metal container, which she perhaps placed in a cloth bag; she must have struggled to keep it well away from her legs to avoid being burnt on her way home. Anyway, the hot ashes were transferred into a special copper basin called 'il braciere' (the brazier), which was then placed inside the circle cut out in the centre of a round wooden platform, around which we sat on wooden chairs with our feet resting on it. That is how we kept a little warm, but we still felt the cold on our backs and, of course, if we moved away from il braciere, the rest of the flat was freezing. It was hard getting into a cold bed at night; we certainly had no hot water bottles! That was one of the penalties we had to pay because of our poverty! It was horrendous feeling so cold!

Anyway, I have only the odd memory of that period which followed our return to Chieti. For a few months there was an old person who stayed with us; his bed was placed in one corner of the dining room. I found out later that he was my mother's paternal grandfather, who soon left and went to live near Turin with one of his sons. Unfortunately, he died only three years after moving out. Apparently, they were not too nice to him up there, so he must have died of a broken heart. However, he could not have stayed with us because we had no room for him. It is sad to become a burden in old age! He had been very clever and dynamic throughout his life and did not deserve such an end.

At first, we used to play hide and seek in the flat in the evening. It was fun having so many brothers and sisters, until they grew into teenagers and no longer wanted to play any games. During the day, when the workmen were not there, we used to go and play at the ground where they were building the other blocks of flats. We used to jump out of the second and third floor windows of the new constructions onto piles of sand. There were no health and safety restrictions in those days! We could have hurt ourselves, but my mother left us to our own devices and did not worry. Luckily, we did not break any limbs or even our spines!

Actually, I don't think Italians in the centre and in the

south of the Country are in the habit of respecting Health & Safety rules even now. An example of utter disregard for safety measures happened about ten years ago whilst my husband Steve and I were walking along one of the deserted beaches near Ortona on a sunny October day. Suddenly we came across an expanse of wet sand. When we started walking on it, we began to sink rapidly; luckily, we managed to literally crawl back towards the dry part of the beach. What had happened was that they had been adding the wet sand they had dredged from the seabed to the shrinking beach in order to widen it: the coastline had been disappearing under the rising level of the Adriatic Sea! There was not a single sign or barrier anywhere to warn people not to walk onto the wet sand, which behaved just like 'quicksand'. It was a frightening experience!

Going back to my childhood, I nearly lost my life one day shortly after we moved in and therefore only about five years of age. I slipped whilst sliding down the eight bannisters from the top floor to the ground floor of the block. Thankfully I managed to grab the rail, saving myself from plunging down the narrow stairwell. My brother Vincent, five years older than me, happened to be nearby; he got hold of my arms and dragged me to safety. That was the second time in my short life that I nearly died.

My grandmother Maria Vincenza moved in with us for a while. However, my mother was not happy about the arrangement and was not very nice to her; I am convinced she thought that my grandmother was there to spy on her. In fact, she made it clear to her that she was not welcome, so the poor woman never joined the rest of the family in the dining room; she must have felt really excluded, but took it in her stride. She thankfully was able to spend the days at my uncle Domenico's place, where unfortunately there was no room for her to sleep, hence the need for her to come back to the flat in the evening.

Her bed was in one corner of the Siberia room. There, next to her bed, was also a chest of drawers in which she kept her clothes and her few possessions. On top of the chest she had photos of my grandfather and some of the son she had conceived whilst living with Don Cesare; Filoteo had sadly died aged only seventeen. Again, she never recovered from that tragedy. I used to feel so sorry for her because she never ventured out of the room except to visit the bathroom. Later on, when I had to study well into the night for my Maturita` Classica exams, she used to sit up on a chair next to my desk to keep me company. Every time she fell asleep, I used to exhort her to get into bed, but she used to say "I am not asleep! I am not asleep!" even though she had been snoring loudly!

We continued to be poor and had no shoes to wear. Walking around with bare feet was the norm, until we went to school and then we had one pair of shoes each once a year. The soles of our feet became really hard, I remember! My mother thought she was being clever by measuring the length of our feet with a string, so that the shop keeper could work out what size shoes all six of us needed, thus making it superfluous for us to turn up at the shop. My mother clearly felt she could not have coped with such an expedition, so she left us at home; she would then come back with six pairs of shoes into which we squeezed our feet, even if they were too tight as they usually were, especially as we all had rather wide feet. The result was that we had to make do with shoes which were too small and ended up with blisters, corns and generally very sore feet. Furthermore, that single pair had to last a whole year until the following October when the new school year started, and had to double up as winter and summer shoes!

Fortunately, my father had been apprenticed to a cobbler before becoming a bricklayer, so he had learnt how to do a basic job of patching up holes in shoes and resoling them; he often used to spend the evening in the cellar working on our footwear! I can still remember how uncomfortable and tight those shoes were! It was almost like having our feet bandaged, as they used to do in China up to the beginning of the twentieth century. It was bad enough for my siblings and me to have been 'swaddled' as babies up to the age of nine months: we were wrapped up in a long broad strip of cloth to restrict our movement, with our legs straightened out and our arms by the sides. This practice was believed to make sure that the baby's legs would grow straight and was still used in some parts of Italy in the 1960s. Of course it was nonsense and babies must have found being wrapped up like Egyptian mummies rather uncomfortable.

My feet are rather misshapen, after many years of wearing shoes too small and too narrow. I dreamt of slipping into lovely and comfortable footwear, so I used to gather some cardboard and strings and tried repeatedly to make some sandals. Of course, each time I only managed a couple of steps before they fell apart! I felt so disappointed!

Although I respected and loved my mother to the end - she lived almost to ninety-seven - she was far from being a good mother! Perhaps it wasn't her fault, as she clearly felt overwhelmed by six children to look after and could not manage too well, so her coping strategy was to leave us to our own devices. At some point she even abandoned us to go and live as a housekeeper for six months somewhere in the south of

Italy, leaving us to fend for ourselves.

Not that her absence would have made too much of a difference anyway, as she barely managed to cook us a plate of pasta every day and then went to see her friend nearby to gossip. To be fair, she often added vegetables to the pasta and made a minestrone when she had enough money to go to the market and buy fresh peas or green beans or potatoes. She also bought some fruit, as it was produced locally and it wasn't too expensive, although it was never enough for six hungry mouths!

She was not house-proud at that point in time, but it must have been mainly because she had given up and could not cope with the mess six children produced. However, I am sure we must have been unkempt and unwashed. Also, we certainly did not have a toothbrush to clean our teeth - I bought my first toothbrush at the age of twenty or so! Our saving grace was that we did not have access to sweets, which could have rotted our teeth further.

When I was about nine, at school I was chosen to recite on stage a poem I had written, but I was required to wear a clean white overall - Italian children wear one at school, a bit like a uniform. Mine must have been a shade of grey instead of white, clearly unwashed for weeks. The teacher mentioned that I should ask my mother to wash my overall in time for the recitation. I don't remember what happened then, but I suspect it remained grey!

I was sent to school regularly without any socks and

I remember feeling embarrassed about my bare feet, whilst all the other children in the class looked pristine and reasonably well dressed. I took it upon myself to make some socks by cutting the sleeves off an old jumper and stitching them up at one end. I cannot remember whether I wore them to school or not; I assume I must have done and probably became the laughing stock of the class, as they must have looked ridiculous.

I seemed to be starving all the time. As I said, we were served some pasta, usually once a day, although often it was also on offer for supper. Meat appeared on the table sometimes on Sundays and on special occasions such as Christmas and Easter. My mother used to go to the market, where, in a corner well away from the other stalls, the farmers' wives used to sell live hens, rabbits and ducks. Thinking about it now, it was rather barbaric for my mother to kill the livestock after taking it home, but we never knew any different, so for us it was the norm. However, I could never bring myself to watch her doing the killing, as I did not like to see the animals suffer.

I did not realise how much I love animals until I came to the UK, though. In those days Italians, including my family, did not treat chickens, rabbits, ducks and even cats and dogs too well. For example, my parents acquired Rocky, an Alsatian, as a guard dog when they lived in France, but they kept him chained up and just gave him a bowl of pasta to eat every day. At some point during his short life, Rocky somehow managed to escape and ended up being shot by a local farmer whilst he was devouring one of the farm's chickens. I used to feel so sorry for the poor animal, but there was nothing I could do about it. However, I cannot really blame my parents for not treating poor Rocky with more compassion, as they did not know it was wrong.

Going back to the chickens, rabbits and ducks bought at the market, we were expected to learn how to gut them after removing their feathers, or skin them if that was the case.

The people living in the baronial house behind our block used to keep pigs. They were really rich peasants who had come to live in the city after paying a pittance for the beautiful villa, which its noble owner had lost through gambling. They had sold the land at the front of the villa to the Council, so the four blocks of flats could be built. I remember once or twice going up the grand staircase, entering the spacious hallway and being mesmerised by the beautiful painting which hung on one of the walls: it was of the house in its former glory, with a carriage complete with coachman and two beautiful horses on the long driveway. Shame that the building had now lost all its splendour and looked more like a farmhouse! Going back to the pigs they kept, unfortunately once a year we had to put up with the heart-wrenching squeals of the poor animals being slaughtered: there was clearly nothing humane in the methods they used to kill them. It was horrendous! The villa is no longer there, as it has been replaced by a block of flats.

I loved Christmas and Easter, not so much for the nice food, but because they were the only occasions in the year that my mother seemed happy. She also tended to be melodramatic and superstitious. Once she burst into tears after dropping a bottle of olive oil on the floor because she believed that it would bring her seven years of bad luck. What nonsense!

Yes, Christmas Day was amazing! My mother smiled, my father was at home for a change and we actually received a few small gifts. It was also traditional to buy some special letter paper decorated with religious scenes from the nearest tobacconist (Tobacco shops used to sell - and still do - all sorts of items, including salt, stamps, letter paper, sweets, cigarettes etc.). We used the special writing paper to write to our parents apologising for our misdemeanours and promising to be good and studious. We placed the letters under my father's plate laid upside down on the table before dinner. He pretended not to notice their presence until the end of the meal, when he would hand them back to us and, one by one, we would read aloud all our apologies and promises of future good behaviour; we were rewarded with a few coins.

I supplemented my diet by scouring the ground around the flats for orange peel people had discarded. I was happy when I found some; clearly, I knew nothing about hygiene and germs. Also, apricot kernels were often dropped on the ground; I used to crack them open using a stone and ate the almond-like pip inside.

We never saw a doctor during our childhood years.

I suppose my parents couldn't afford doctors and there was no equivalent of the NHS in Italy. So, when we were ill, we just had to recover spontaneously. The only medication we were offered was a very bitter herb - I cannot remember what it was called - which my older siblings were sent to find on grass verges just outside the city. My mother made some sort of tea out of it and made us drink it mixed with milk. It was horrendous! I still remember its awful taste! So, if it wasn't bad enough being ill, we also had to swallow that disgusting potion. Furthermore, I have since discovered that I am lactose-intolerant, like most people in Italy, so milk would have caused digestive problems which would have made me feel even worse.

We were lucky to survive all the childhood illnesses

without any vaccinations, except for the Smallpox vaccine. The first time I was vaccinated against Tetanus and Rubella was in the UK, when I was expecting my son.

Another memory of the time after we moved into the flat has haunted me all my life! My father was a bit of a Don Juan and apparently was having an affair with my mother's best friend, Dora. Mind you, my mother was not an angel of rectitude and she too apparently had several affairs. In this incident, when my mother confronted my father about the liaison, they had a terrible argument, during which he tried to pick her up and throw her out of the dining room window. We were on the fourth floor! Thankfully she managed to get away. I believe that my father must have had too much to drink on that occasion, as he was not an aggressive man at all. Indeed, I never witnessed him using any violence against anyone else, neither did I ever see him drunk. However, that time it all happened before my eyes- I often thought that it was a horrendous thing to do in the presence of such a young child!

Of course, we had no toys to play with. When I was seven or eight, I was given two very small dolls, which must have been, at the most, five inches long. I was delighted with them and was very maternal towards them, trying to make little clothes and bedding for them. I used to sit just outside the flats, in a shaded area, and spent hours on my own playing with those tiny dolls. In the immediate neighbourhood there were no other little girls I could play with unfortunately, except one, Rosa, who was rarely allowed out.

I used to be fascinated by the farmers' wives going by, from the small farms just outside Chieti to the fruit and vegetable market up the road. They used to balance enormous wicker baskets on their heads, often holding them with just one hand or not at all, after placing a rolled tea towel in the shape of a ring under them, so that their base would not feel too hard and uncomfortable. I used to spend hours trying to emulate those women, carrying objects on my head. Unfortunately, that did not do any good to my cervical spine!

Prior to the dolls, I loved to go and play with a little boy who lived in one of the flats opposite. It was the highlight of my day, as he let me ride his tricycle. It was such an exhilarating feeling to zip around the dining room table on that little trike! My dream of owning such a toy never became reality. However, I don't remember ever feeling envious of anyone for having what I did not have!

I made do with collecting bits of paper, especially discarded sweet wrappers, little stones and twigs and pretending to be a shop keeper, letting my imagination transport me into a world where I was happy and contented. However, since I have become an adult, I have been saddened by the realisation that my childhood was hard and neglected. I don't agree with those psychologists who might say that I was lucky to be so poor, as that must have made me tough. I think the deprivation and neglect robbed me of my childhood and it was not fair. The early years in someone's life should be carefree and leave a warm feeling inside, with happy memories and lots of love all around. Mine were cold, deprived, neglected and hard. Of course, I can identify with all the children who suffer poverty and hardship in the world and I wish I could stop all that! It is just not right and not fair.

When I became a mother, I tried to compensate for what my mother lacked, therefore I showered my children with love, affection and plenty of books and toys - maybe even too many - to make sure they had the childhood I never had. Maybe it was too much the other way, but I don't regret anything I have done for my children.

During my childhood years we never celebrated our

birthdays. In fact, I hated them, as it was traditional for anyone else who knew to get hold of both our ear lobes and pull them hard, whilst saying 'Buon Compleanno!' I don't know where the custom came from, but it was horrible.

Above my top lip there is a scar, left by the injury I received when I fell off a chair on which I was standing in order to do the washing up at the kitchen sink. Unfortunately, the chair had lost the middle section of the woven fabric which had covered it, so I was standing on it with my feet either side of the hole. It is not surprising that a five-year-old ended up injuring herself in those circumstances - I sometimes think it was pure luck that I managed to survive my childhood!

Although we could see the Adriatic Sea from the

windows of the flat and it was only about ten kms away, we never went there whilst I was growing up, except for a couple of times, when my sister Lucina, who was seven years older than me and often looked after her younger siblings, organised a trip to the nearest beach in Francavilla.

Unfortunately, we did not know anything about the damaging rays of the sun, so we all went home terribly burnt after spending the day lying on the sand without a parasol, which we could not afford to hire. I don't think sun cream even existed! In any case, we would not have been able to buy any! No wonder I have been battling skin cancer (Actinic Keratosis) on my face for years! To top it all off, for our picnic on the beach my sister prepared sandwiches thickly spread with lashings of lard - and nothing else. She thought she would treat us, as lard was better than olive oil. How wrong she was!

CHAPTER 3

MY SCHOOL DAYS

I don't remember much about my days spent at primary school, except the dirty overall incident and one or two other snippets. I started school aged six and a half; we had to be six in order to qualify for a place.

Interestingly, primary education had been compulsory in Italy as early as 1859. Also, the leaving age was raised to fourteen in 1923. In spite of this, there was widespread illiteracy; in fact, 80% of the population was unable to read and write at that time, especially in rural areas of the centre and south of Italy. People just did not send their children to school, whatever the law said! By the end of the 19th century, that percentage had halved, but it was still not ideal.

My paternal grandmother Maria Vincenza, as I stated earlier, was indeed illiterate. Later on, during my teenage years, she wanted so much to learn to read that she often asked me to teach her. Unfortunately, in my immaturity, I used to laugh at her with her monosyllabic reading, so she gave up trying. It is one of my regrets that I never helped her to become literate.

Both my parents could read and write, though, as they had been sent to school for three years. My father was extremely clever, so it was a real shame that he was never given the opportunity to study. I am sure he could have become perhaps a lawyer or a doctor if he had had a good education, but it wasn't to be! Later on, he used to read all our school textbooks, so his general knowledge became excellent. He also learnt by heart several salient verses of La DIVINA COMMEDIA (The Divine Comedy), by Dante Alighieri, the Italian equivalent of Shakespeare. He was able to recite them faultlessly up to his death at the age of ninety-two.

Coming back to my primary school days, I am convinced that I had to walk to school on my own from day one because I don't remember anybody else ever walking with me. My primary school was an imposing building situated about half a mile from the flat. I remember calling once for my friend Rosa, who was one year older than me, and asking her to walk to school with me. She said she wasn't going! We know that the law was not enforced, so people like her never bothered with education.

I also remember sitting, aged nine, an oral exam. The title of the text I was asked to read was 'La Quercia Caduta' (The Fallen Oak Tree). I got confused about the pronunciation of the 'Q' and read it as a 'G'. I made the mistake twice, but then I corrected myself and sailed through the rest of the exam. My marks were all nine out of ten throughout, as I seemed to be quite bright (even if I say so myself!). In fact, I was the only member of my family to go to university; however, all my siblings ended up doing well and achieving a good standard of living in spite of their lack of educational qualifications.

When the exam results were displayed on a board in the entrance of the school building, as it was customary, I was again left to my own devices and had to walk there alone. On the way back I remember meeting an uncle who came to visit us whilst he was in Italy for NATO operations, serving in the American Army in 1951. I proudly showed him the piece of paper on which I had copied my excellent exam results. Uncle Alfonso Junior was the son of my grandmother Maria Vincenza's brother, also called Alfonso, who had emigrated to the States when he was only fourteen years old. When he returned to Pittsburgh, USA, Alfonso Junior sent us a parcel, containing some delicious chocolate bars and some pretty dresses. Unfortunately, he only did that once, but clearly it must have been expensive to send us that one parcel! I thought his was an amazing gesture and made me so happy, because for once I had some beautiful dresses to wear instead of rags.

At the end of primary school I went with my mother to a photographer to have my photo taken for the first time in my life, as it was needed to enrol at the middle school. I was eleven and had never been photographed before then. In the photo I think I looked small for my age and almost emaciated; this is not surprising, considering the starvation and neglect I suffered. I will never know what I looked like before the age of eleven. How sad! My four older siblings had been photographed before the war started, but pictures were understandably not a priority for my parents during those difficult years. The only thing I know is that I had lots of ringlets, which one of the neighbours said bobbed up and down when I ran; consequently, my nickname was 'Ricciolina' (Little Curls).

I continued to show academic promise in the middle school, which I attended for three years. At fourteen, I had to make a choice, as we had to decide in which direction I wanted to go with my studies. My teachers were impressed with my performance and advised my parents to enrol me at the local liceo classico. The school was located in a very old building right in the town centre and was steeped in history, with shiny marble floors and great architecture; the classrooms had very high ceilings and were almost intimidating because of their vastness.

Mussolini had emphasised the importance of classically oriented schools such as the liceo classico, because his goal was to educate the future upper classes. Unfortunately, I just ended up feeling inferior to my classmates, as they came from well-to-do families with luxurious homes and expensive clothes: for example, one of them was a baroness, another was the son of the Mayor! Suffice to say that I never invited any of them back to my humble dwelling, where poverty and squalor were very obvious.

Greek was my forte. In exams it was customary to help others in the class, as teachers turned a blind eye and condoned a little cheating. In the Maturita` Classica exams, for example, after I finished my translation from Greek into Italian, I produced a copy which was circulated amongst my class mates, who were extremely grateful. At the time, I did not see anything wrong in doing that, as it was what everyone did! I can now see that it wasn't right though!

There was another girl in my class who also came from more humble origins than all the other students: her name is Elena and she became my good friend for life. We are still in touch. The difference between her and me, though, was that her mother and father were farmers who were not short of money and were excellent parents to her and her sister Antonietta. They were also very nice to me and often invited me to go and spend a few days at their farmhouse. Each time I enjoyed the visit very much and especially loved the home-made bread toasted on the open fire in the kitchen and which was particularly tasty rubbed with fresh garlic and sprinkled with a few drops of olive oil. Delicious!

Elena's mother, a sweet little lady, was uneducated and also rather naïve; we used to laugh at her innocent remarks! For example, once she told me that they had acquired a donkey, so she invited me to go and see it down in the fields. Unfortunately, for some reason, the donkey happened not to be where she thought it would be, so, on the way back, when she saw somebody else's donkey going by, she pointed to it and declared "Look, Anna. Our donkey looks exactly like that one!" She assumed that I did not know what a donkey looked like! Later on, when I visited them with my first husband, Denis, an Englishman, she exclaimed "What a shame! He is a handsome young man, but he does not know how to speak properly! And you, Anna, how come you can no longer speak properly either?" She had heard us speak English and interpreted that as a speech impediment! She was not too bright, but quite delightful.

I have to thank my parents, in spite of all their shortcomings, for allowing me to get an education. In fact, every year they had to buy all the textbooks, which was a massive expense. Although education was compulsory, as we said, parents had to find the money to purchase all the necessary textbooks and equipment. Thankfully, at this stage my father was earning a little more money and could just about afford to pay for all the books in monthly instalments. One day I asked my mother for the money I needed to buy an urgent textbook I required for my homework from the local bookshop. We ended up having an argument, as she said she only had enough money to buy food for that day. I shouted that the book was more important than food! She won the argument and I ended up getting a bad mark for not doing my homework.

The reason we had nothing to eat in the morning was due mainly to the fact that breakfast was not considered too important in Italy and people just drank an espresso, usually at the nearest bar. So, we went to school on an empty stomach. Fortunately, my grandmother Maria Vincenza was there to help during my teenage years. Although she had lived with us after the war, at that point in time she had moved out to live with my uncle Domenico, who had acquired a bigger flat and had now room for her to stay. She used to intercept us on the way to school and handed over a bun.

At first, I accepted the buns, but when I went to the liceo classico, I felt terribly embarrassed by her presence in case my classmates saw me receiving food, so I hid from her. I am sure she saw me trying to avoid her; it must have been hurtful! I wish I had not done that! Again, I will always regret my actions, but teenagers often have little empathy for others and I did not understand that I wasn't being nice.

I feel that my education was not really great and my general knowledge was very poor, even after thirteen years spent at school; that is because of the way the Italian education system worked. I fear that things have not much improved even now. Instead of actually teaching lessons, my teachers used to set homework which entailed learning the contents of a certain

number of pages from a textbook. In the lesson they simply did what was called 'interrogazioni', that is to say that they would call a couple of pupils to stand by the teacher's desk, either side and they would test them orally on the contents of the pages set for homework the previous lesson. Those marks given would count towards the final percentage at the end of the year and they would decide whether the student could go into the higher year group or fail the year and repeat it the following October. There was also the chance to sit an exam in September in a maximum of three subjects. If they went well, then the pupil would pass into the next year group.

What a waste of my youth! My life centred around going to school and then going home to spend the rest of the day doing homework! I was never given the opportunity to learn sports and to find out whether I had aptitude for tennis, for example. Sadly, we only had one hour of PE a week and in that, we simply learnt how to march like soldiers! We were also set so much learning by rote. This took a lot of time and energy, so I would go to bed really early in the evening, usually at about eight o'clock in the spring and even earlier in the winter; I would then set the alarm for four or five o'clock in the morning, so I could learn all the poetry and verses I had been asked to memorise. The sunrises over she sea were stunning, though! The Adriatic shimmered in the distance: it was a truly amazing sight and witnessing its magic made getting up so early more bearable.

In winter, coming up to Christmas, I could hear the bagpipes being played on the farms scattered just outside Chieti. It was traditional to pay a nominal sum to shepherds who came down from remote mountain villages to earn some money playing the bagpipes to celebrate Christmas. They even came into the town and occasionally performed for us too; they used to turn up, usually in the early evening and played a short burst of their bagpipes outside the front door of the flat. They must have been exhausted by the time the evening came, as they started so early in the morning, the poor souls.

A drawback of my early morning studying was that there was no food in the flat and my mother was usually nowhere to be found, as she was busy gossiping at the neighbour's place. So, as a teenager, I used to go to bed on an empty stomach! If you think that no breakfast was ever provided, I was surviving on one plate of pasta a day, at a time when I would have needed good quality nourishment instead. How sad!

My mother occasionally must have felt bad about the situation, so once or twice she made sure I would get a sort of 'zabaglione'- a raw egg yolk, whisked with sugar, which all other parents gave their teenagers as a tonic. This would have given me iron and vitamin A, which my body would have badly needed. Unfortunately, that only happened a few times and then she went back to her usual neglect. She did have a favourite child, though: it was my sister Rita (four years older than me), who was secretly given the best food and morsels; in fact, she grew quite tall and is enjoying good health even now, unlike my short stature, clearly due to lack of essential nourishment, and my present poor health, including the low density of my bones which is causing problems with my spine.

I should have never been made to attend the liceo classico, as, after the five years there, I felt I had not accomplished anything unless I went to University. I should have studied at the scuola magistrale (school for primary teachers) instead, as I would have gained a teaching diploma, which would have given me the chance to teach at primary level at the age of nineteen. A missed opportunity! My life could have panned out differently. Who knows! I had to wait more than another decade before achieving my ambition of becoming a teacher and finally earn a living. Interestingly, now primary school teachers in Italy also need to go to university and gain a degree.

CHAPTER 4

MY FIRST VISIT TO FRANCE

My father started off as a bricklayer, but he became so good at his job and expanded his skills in his trade so much, that he decided to start building houses himself with the help of a friend, who had worked with him for a number of years. However, he never really made enough money to live on, as he was too honest and did not charge enough, in spite of the fact that he used the best materials; so eventually he went bankrupt! Disillusioned, he decided to join all the men who were trying their luck abroad. At the time, in the fifties, there was nearly a mass exodus from Italy towards Argentina, France and other countries, including Australia. My father eventually arranged to go and work in France, specifically in Lyon. I still remember his departure in 1955 or so: he knelt in front of my grandmother, who placed her hand over his head and gave him her blessing. They were both crying!

I was not too upset by his departure, as I was not close to him and I was used to his absence from home. However, I knew that he was a good man and a good father, in spite of his occasional affairs. It wasn't his fault that he had to be an absent father and that my older brothers went off the rails because they did not have him there to guide them.

In France, my father lived at first in a wooden hut on a building site so that he could save most of his money to send back to us in Italy. He also put aside enough to buy a piece of land in a village near Lyon called

Lucenay, with the intention of building a house there. He eventually did just that. However, he first built a shack on the land and promptly invited two of my brothers to go and join him. My mother had got to the stage where she was unable to control my two older brothers, who were constantly truanting and getting into trouble both at home and at school. Things were getting out of hand, as once or twice my mother threw a knife in their direction when they answered back. She always did that as a joke, laughing about it, but I thought her behaviour was crazy; that frightened me greatly and I was afraid that one of my brothers would get hurt! Thankfully my father had found jobs for both of them. My brother Domenico still lives in France and can be described as a proper Frenchman in every sense of the word. My other brother sadly passed away twenty-seven years ago with lung cancer due to his smoking. Everybody smoked in those days and people were not aware of the dangers to health from tobacco!

From the age of fifteen, I started spending my summer holidays (which stretched from the beginning of June to October) in France. We travelled on steam trains, overnight. I can still remember vividly the soothing rhythmic sounds of the engines, occasionally punctuated by whistles. I loved going along with that cacophony of amazing sounds which belong to a bygone era, as travelling on modern trains is a completely different - not so romantic – experience. We could not afford couchettes, so we arrived in Lyon completely drained after a journey of nearly twenty-four hours. I loved France, the French and their beautiful language, which I picked up quite quickly. I also earned my very first pocket money ever and had my first crush on a French lad called Antoine. It was very innocent and totally platonic. We didn't even exchange a kiss!

I was invited, with my sister Rita and my brother Franco, to go and help harvest the grapes on Antoine's family farm. The whole activity was back-breaking, but so enjoyable. I loved every minute of it. Antoine and I worked together either side of the vine, each with a bucket in which we would drop the bunches of grapes; they were for wine making, so we could be rough with them. Antoine and I would always finish the row first, as we worked very fast, ahead of all the others. I also loved the food that Antoine's mother prepared for us. We had breakfast after a couple of hours' work; we enjoyed delicious baguettes with French salami, chocolate or goat's cheese. Of course, there was wine galore, but I never drank any. I had seen my maternal grandfather lying on the ground drunk outside his house once when I was quite young; he also vomited repeatedly and ranted in an unintelligible language. That pitiful sight was enough to put me off alcohol for life, so I have never been drunk in my life. Actually, I don't like alcohol at all.

Back to the 'vendanges' (grape harvesting)! After a morning's work, we had lunch comprising several courses. The evening meal was just as substantial as lunch. French cuisine is absolutely amazing! It was all so delicious and the food was so different from the pasta I was served at home! At the end of the week, we received our francs. It was an incredible feeling to be earning some money, as in Italy there was no work of any kind available to teenagers. After returning to Chieti, Antoine and I wrote to each other, in French of course, and we rekindled our platonic love affair the following year. Then, two years later, by now in the last year at school, I met Niny and I was no longer interested in Antoine.

Niny was three years older than me and a law student at Bari University, but was earning pin-money in Chieti by tutoring some boarders at a private school situated next door to the liceo classico. Meeting him was all consuming: he was so romantic and charming and totally won me over. He seemed to really be my soul mate at the time; he was also handsome and very clever and became a judge later on, although he died, aged thirty-seven, in suspicious circumstances.

After spending a year working in Chieti, Niny went back to his small town not far from Bari; that is when things started to turn sour between us. I discovered later that he was going out with numerous other girls whilst I stayed in Chieti. We used to write to each other every day and I never suspected any wrong-doings on his part, until I was invited to go and stay with his family for a few days. There his behaviour rang alarm bells, as he often made excuses to go out in the evening, leaving me at home with his mother and sister. One day I decided to investigate the contents of a locked drawer in his writing desk, which I prised open. It was a shock to find love letters and photographs of several other girls! The reality hit me that he was a rat and could not be trusted. He also seemed to be very keen to get rid of me and kept asking when I intended to go back to Chieti.

One day I let him take me to the railway station in the nearby village. He left without waiting for my train to arrive, which I thought was suspicious, so I made the decision to go back to his house instead of getting the train and see whether I would catch him 'in flagrante' with some other girl. Unfortunately, as it was late afternoon, there were no more coaches going to his village that day.

A short and tubby man, of around forty years of age, with very dark hair, was there with his two children. He approached when he saw me sitting there, disconsolate, and asked me what the problem was. He offered to give me a lift to Niny's village on his Lambretta scooter, which he then proceeded to fetch from his house; I felt reassured by the fact that I had gone with him to his house and had spoken to his wife, who had no objections, so I climbed on the back seat of his Lambretta and off we went. By the time we left, it was already dark, as it was winter and the days were shorter. The road to Niny's village was very straight and stretched for a good twenty miles.

After a short while, I became suspicious, as the scooter's engine seemed to stop. When questioned, the man just said it had broken down and we should walk. He tried to convince me to walk near the kerb, but I was not stupid and made a point of walking on the road instead; presumably his plan was to push me to the ground and rape me. I dread to think what else he had in mind!

It was very scary to be there, in the middle of nowhere, in complete darkness and isolation with that stranger. The sky was cloudy, so there were no stars nor moon and the only occasional light came from one or two cars which were cruising the opposite direction. It was all so surreal, as if I was having a bad dream! I kept begging him to try the engine again, which he eventually did.

It worked, as there was clearly nothing wrong with it! So, we got back onto the scooter and continued down the road. Alas, my suspicions were confirmed when, literally a few seconds later, he could not control himself any longer and made his intentions very clear: he stretched one of his arms towards me and grabbed one of my breasts! Without any hesitation - and without thinking that I could have hurt myself really badly, but it was a case of choosing the lesser of the two evils - I jumped off the scooter and fell onto the road, scraping my knees and elbows on the rough surface. It could have been a lot worse! I picked myself up, ran to the other side of the road and flagged down a car coming the other way; fortunately, the car stopped and I climbed in. I briefly told the young man at the wheel what had happened and asked him to be kind enough to give me a lift to Niny's house. However, although he did just that, at first he tried to convince me to go to a hotel with him instead! 'Frying pans' and 'fires' came to mind, but I had no choice other than trust him to deliver me safely to the address I had given him.

Mine was a very lucky escape! I regret not reporting the nasty incident to the Police, but I had had enough of it all at that point and just wanted to go home to Chieti. Also, I felt ashamed of my utter stupidity and naivety and did not want to talk about it. I arrived at Niny's house all scratched and bruised, but no one tried to find out what had happened to me. Niny was not there of course! When I told his mother that I knew he had other girlfriends, she replied that I was the girl he wanted to marry, so I should not care about his escapades! That was the mentality in the south of Italy in those days: the man should sow his wild oats and his wife/ girlfriend should accept it without even batting an eyelid.

I resolved not to put up any longer with Niny's shenanigans. Something died in me that night, alongside my trust for the man, and that was the end of my relationship with him. I no longer felt any emotion towards him. It is strange how an all-consuming passion can end so suddenly! But it did.

Later on, after he got married to one of his other girlfriends and had two children, but was clearly unhappy, he tried to contact me again in order to rekindle the relationship, but it was too late. He told me that he had never stopped loving me and could not forget me. He also said he had kept a pair of my shoes and a nightdress I had left at his house as mementos; the two items were locked in his desk at work. He died shortly after that. Apparently, he had transferred his family to the very north of Italy to escape the Mafia, as he had been threatened after convicting one of its members when he worked as a judge. He did not give me any more details, but he said that the Mafia had burned his villa at his seaside resort and was hunting him to seek revenge. Suddenly, out of the blue, he died on one of his visits back to his village. His family refused to elaborate on the cause of his death, so I will never know what happened to him. Presumably they too were afraid of incurring the wrath of the Mafia!

At the end of my last year at the liceo classico I sat those extremely difficult final exams called 'Maturita` Classica' - believe it or not - equivalent to eight A' Levels. Recently they have reduced the number of subjects to just three, as they have recognised that the traditional exam was just too hard. Afterwards I enrolled at Bari University to study Classical Languages. I had chosen Bari because Niny studied there; that was clearly before I found out about his infidelities. In Italy it is not always necessary to attend lectures in some subjects, so I mostly studied from home in Chieti; however, I used to travel to Bari to sit exams.

At some point I thought I would get a little job in Bari, so I worked as a secretary to a lawyer. I don't think that job was meant for me; I hated it and was not very good at it, so I did not do it for very long and went back home after just a couple of months. I was also paid a pittance and it wasn't worth my time and energy.

When I ended my relationship with Niny, I

transferred to Urbino University (not far from Rimini), in the Marche region, although I never completed the course there, as I started teaching at first and then my life changed direction.

At that point I was living with my lovely grandmother in Chieti, as the rest of the family had gone to live in France. There was a shortage of teachers in middle and secondary schools at the time, so they used to appoint university students on temporary teaching contracts. However, one needed a contact and to know someone influential in order to be considered. I am afraid it all worked - and still does! - like that in Italy: there is a lot of nepotism and corruption in every area, except perhaps in the northern regions. My uncle knew the man who organised the temporary contracts, so I was lucky to get one of the teaching posts for two years in a row.

I taught in Abruzzo in middle schools. During the first year it was in a place called Villalfonsina. It was the year John F. Kennedy was assassinated; everybody remembers where they were when they heard the tragic news. I was on my way to the school! The second year I taught in a village situated at the very foot of the Maiella called Fara San Martino, the place where they make the famous 'De Cecco' pasta. It seems that the water which gushes out of the mountain is the reason why the 'De Cecco' pasta tastes so good. I actually taught one of the De Cecco girls. Her parents brought me a lovely gift one day: it was a colourful, home-made throw made of wool, which would have been rather expensive to buy. However, I declined it because I thought it amounted to a form of bribery; it was silly of me, as I am sure it was just meant as a thank-you gift, the Italian equivalent of 'an apple for the teacher'. I had become rather cynical and no longer trusted people. Previously, when I taught at Villalfonsina, the children would often go out in the countryside to find some wild asparagus, which they brought to me together with freshly laid eggs: a really lovely gesture from my pupils.

At the end of that year, my loneliness became so unbearable and I missed my family so much, that I decided to leave Italy and move to France. A new chapter of my life began.

CHAPTER 5

MY MOVE TO FRANCE

So, I no longer wanted to stay in Chieti because of my extreme loneliness. There were still many prejudices in those days and a young woman had a very restricted lifestyle and could not really go anywhere on her own. Also, if you had had a boyfriend, you suddenly became 'soiled goods' and other young men were not interested in you: the Abruzzi mentality was very archaic in those days and did not make my life easy.

The time had come for me to go and join my family in France! My grandmother was devastated about losing me, so she tried all sorts of strategies in order to keep me there with her, including acquiring a couple of kittens, which sadly got sick and died. She was working in the local cemetery as a grave cleaner: people gave her the task of keeping the tombs of their loved ones clean and tidy. I discovered later that she had that little job in order to make ends meet, as she provided me with food, but I never realised that I should have contributed financially. I could have easily done that, as I had been teaching for two years and earned good money, but I was very immature and I just did not understand, wrapped up in my own self-pity!

One day, in 1964, I left with a few clothes in a suitcase. My grandmother waved to me out of one of the windows of the flat. Before disappearing round the corner, I looked up and saw that she was crying inconsolably. Of course, at the time I did not know that I would not see her ever again: she sadly died two years later.

When I arrived in Lucenay, I loved the family atmosphere in the house my father was still building. I no longer felt lonely and thought I would stay there for the rest of my life. I also loved my eighteen-month old nephew called Stefan, as my sister Rita - who had moved to France two years earlier after completing five years at Art school - had married and had her first child. Stefan was a beautiful little boy, with blond hair, very bright and full of life. I loved spending time playing with him; I even took him to Lyon zoo a few times. After suffering so much solitude in Chieti, I was delighted to have a child around to keep me busy.

Also, as every member of the family was now working - even my mother - there was no shortage of money; the house had all the necessary comforts, including a big TV set. In Italy we never had enough money to buy one of those, as the prices were astronomical at the time, so we used to go to the neighbour's flat to watch the occasional American drama such as 'Perry Mason' with Raymond Burr, with Italian subtitles of course.

I decided to start a degree course in Maths at Lyon University; I wanted a change from Greek and Latin, but I found it all rather difficult, so I transferred to the top-level course in French Language and Civilisation. There I met students of all nationalities and even a

Japanese lad, who apparently wanted to marry me. His family, taking his intentions seriously, made sure he did not follow that foolish plan and sent a young woman, who was his official fiancé in Japan, to Lyon; they got married immediately and I was invited to the wedding! Interestingly, I did not feel romantically inclined towards him and had not realised that he had told his family about me and that he wanted to marry me!

I passed the French course, which lasted a year, with flying colours. My intention was then to get a job in Lyon, possibly as a bilingual secretary and to settle in France. But it wasn't to be! I soon found that my freedom was also restricted living with my family in Lucenay. There was still the idea that an unmarried young woman should stay at home as much as possible and be chaperoned when out; furthermore, her brothers had a say on her actions.

It all came to a head one Sunday, when my sister's family and my brother Domenico and his wife and son came over to lunch. Immediately after coffee was served, my younger brother Franco suggested we both went dancing in the village nearby, as there was some sort of festival there and it was traditional to dance in the square; they used to cordon off a section of the centre of the village and charged a fee to enter. When I started getting ready in my bedroom, my brother Domenico came to see me - spurred on by my mother, undoubtedly - and told me that I should be ashamed of myself for wanting to go dancing instead of washing up and clearing the table! It was like being in the Middle

Ages! Also, it was about time I learnt to cook, he said, since I was not even capable of preparing the pasta sauce, unlike his friend's daughter, Lucia, who was younger than me and could make delicious lasagna. What he did not say was that Lucia had not spent so many years studying and had learnt to be a housewife instead. I could not believe my ears when I heard all that, so I burst into tears, pondering what I should do next.

It became clear in my mind that I could not go back to Italy, because of the soul-destroying solitude I had suffered, nor could I stay in France, with my freedom so terribly curtailed and having to be at the mercy of my brother, who thought he had jurisdiction over me simply because I was a single woman. I was twenty-four years old, for goodness sake - I was not a teenager! I decided that coming to England was my only course of action.

One of my university friends, Carlos, was coming to the UK to learn English. He had already spent a year in Germany, then one year in France, both times with the purpose of learning the local language, so he intended to go to Oxford in September that year, 1966. He exhorted me to join him, but I was rather reluctant at first, as it was a big step and the fact that I did not speak a single word of English really worried me. I had watched some films in English and thought that I would never be able to understand such a difficult language, which was totally different from French and Italian. It is only later that I discovered that over forty-five thousand

English words have a Latin root, so the two languages are more similar than I ever imagined!

After the dancing episode, I contacted Carlos, who promised to find me a placement as an au pair in Oxford, where he was an entertainer singing and playing his guitar in one of the restaurants. He kept his promise and soon put me in touch with an agency which found me a family: Mr Gilbert was a hairdresser and his wife was a student teacher at Westminster College near Oxford. They were interested in me working for them because I already had a driving licence - I had used some of the money I had earned teaching on driving lessons- and I was twenty-four, so mature enough to look after their two young children, Michelle, seven, and David, five. Mrs Gilbert found it especially convenient having me there, as she was a learner driver and could practise driving on the way to Westminster College in the morning; I would then drive the car back to the house. Ironically, Westminster College is where I ended up studying to become a qualified teacher of French.

When I received the invitation to go and stay with the English family in North Oxford, I announced to my family that I would be leaving shortly for England to study English -- I said that my intention was to stay only three months and then return to France.

Meanwhile, something else happened to reinforce my conviction that I had to leave for England! At the beginning of October, they would put up the most amazing illuminations in the Old Lyon. As my friends were all going out in the evening to see the lights in the old town, I decided to go too. I had warned my mother that I would be returning late that evening, on the last coach which left Lyon at around 22.30. In fact, I returned at the time I had indicated and had to walk the last one hundred yards or so from the bus stop to the house, in the isolation and complete darkness which enveloped the country road - the house was situated outside the village, in a rather remote area with few other dwellings around it. I was very scared to be walking back on my own at that time of the evening! That was bad enough, but I did not foresee what awaited me when I returned to the house. I unlocked the front door and was shocked to find my mother appearing before me; I had not even had the chance to step inside! She pointed her finger at me and growled

"What time do you call this. Puttana!" (Whore) That was a word my mother used freely and often - nevertheless, it hurt, because all I had done was to go and see the illuminations. I was totally innocent: I had done nothing wrong!

If, until then, I had any doubts about going to England, they were certainly dispelled by this unpleasant episode and I felt I had no choice but leave! To top it all off, I had another problem to resolve. After my French course at the University had ended, I had found a way to earn some money by travelling with groups of young people from France to Italy as their guide during the summer months. I accompanied two groups on two separate occasions in August. When the second trip came to an end at the beginning of

September 1966, we returned to France via Florence. In fact, we arrived there two days before torrential rain flooded that beautiful city and endangered lots of its artistic treasures; we thankfully only spent one night there before the flooding occurred.

The first group was delightful and we got on very well; afterwards they made me honorary member of their village near Toulouse for life. However, there was one problem: I suspected that their priest had taken a shine to me. After the trip, we corresponded frequently; his behaviour and letters were always more than correct, but my intuition told me that all was not as it should be and I was sure he was romantically interested in me. He was not your typical Catholic priest anyway, as he shunned cassocks and dressed in jeans and   t-shirts instead. Sometime in late October he mentioned the possibility of coming to Lucenay to visit me, but I did not feel at ease with the idea. Mind you, I don't know why Catholic priests are not allowed to get married like those in other Churches. Surely it is unnatural to be celibate for life: having a wife and children would help them understand more about the ways of the world.

So that was that - I had to go away! Interestingly, there was no objection from my parents about me travelling alone all the way to England, although they wanted to restrict my movements when I lived there. It was a total contradiction! The absurdities were also evident when they did not mind me waiting all alone at the bus stop, which was basically in the middle of nowhere and therefore hardly safe for me, when I eventually left for the UK.

Indeed, one November evening my brother Franco gave me a lift to the bus stop at about seven o' clock. Being winter, cold and with an extremely thick fog enveloping the whole area, the road was completely deserted. My brother had no intention of hanging about and returned home immediately after dropping me off. The coach was not due for another thirty minutes! There I was, standing on a country road rendered practically invisible by the thickest fog imaginable, shivering because of the cold, but also for fear of the unknown. I tried to muster the necessary courage I needed to travel to a foreign country about which I knew nothing and whose language I did not understand. The coach arrived more than one hour late because of the poor visibility, so I had to spend what seemed an eternity in that desolate solitude, lost in a sea of dense fog. I felt alone in the world! However, I tried to overcome my sense of despair by reminding myself that I had no choice but leave and hope for the best.

When I arrived at the station in Lyon, I had to wait several hours before boarding the train for Paris, which did not leave until one o'clock in the morning. On the train, the compartments were full. Unfortunately, there was a young chap who sat next to me and whose hands wandered the moment the main lights were turned off so that people could sleep - I clearly hated it and had to keep slapping him. I don't know why I attracted that sort of behaviour! At one point I even walked along the corridor to check the other compartments, but there was no room anywhere else, so I just stood there until first light; I had been unable to relax because of that pest next to me.

In Paris, I had to travel by Metro to the Gare du Nord. Eventually the train left for Calais, where we boarded a boat bound for Dover. In 1966 it was very difficult to be allowed entry into the UK. I was interviewed by the British Immigration officers for at least an hour- it turned out to be a bit like the Spanish Inquisition! They did not leave any stones unturned and especially wanted to know why I wanted to enter the UK; did I want to work as a bilingual secretary, did I have any contacts in England who could help me if I needed assistance of any kind etc. Fortunately, the sister of one of my aunts lived in Birmingham and her brother lived in Kidderminster, so Immigration reluctantly allowed me to enter the country. The whole interrogation was exhausting and had to be conducted in French, as I still did not speak a single word of English at that stage.

When we landed at Dover, I saw the white cliffs and thought how beautiful this country was. Immediately I fell in love with the rows of little houses with red roof tiles; it all looked so different from Italy and France, where people lived mainly in apartment blocks. It was also so incredibly verdant. I had loved France, but I felt completely at home in a country which looked clean, tidy, disciplined and where people seemed very keen to help me.

I had been completely unprepared for such a journey and for me it was all new. Thankfully, after getting on the train bound for London, some kind passengers who spoke French explained that we would arrive at Victoria station and that I would need to take the underground to Paddington in order to catch a train going to Oxford, my final destination. I just about managed to negotiate the underground and boarded a train to Oxford, where I took a taxi to the address Carlos had given me.

The friends with whom he was sharing the house were mainly Spanish speaking. There I had my first taste ever of a cup of tea with milk- I thought it was delicious; until that point, I had always drunk tea with lemon, both in Italy and France. It was quite a discovery! Later on I convinced my mother to try it and she too loved it. I also had my first encounter with Marmite; again, I loved it and still think its taste is amazing.

A few days later I met the family in North Oxford and I soon moved in with them. Six unhappy months followed, as I felt exploited and taken for granted. They lived in a three-bedroom semi and had no spare room for me, so they placed a single bed in their dining room: it wasn't really comfortable, as I had to continue living out of my suitcase, with no cupboard or chest for my belongings. However, the arrangement would not have been too bad, had they not asked me to vacate the room on Sundays so that they could have lunch there.

I was very unhappy about that: Sundays were my only day off and I would have preferred it if I could have stayed in bed the only time in the week I did not have to get up at seven o'clock. I became furious about this and did not think it was at all fair: I thought they should have never employed an au pair if they did not have a room which would allow her to have her own space.

Also, I was instructed to clean and tidy the house from top to bottom every single day, six times a week, as well as baby-sit and take the children to school and back most days. My other tasks were to cook, once a week, beef mince in tomato sauce the Italian way - I had to improvise the recipe- and accompany Mrs Gilbert to Westminster College, in the car, on the days she was there.

So I did my chores, performed my other duties and then left the house to go and spend time with some friends of Carlos, with whom I communicated in Spanish or French, as my English was still non-existent, due to the fact that I never had a chance to practise and use it with the family. I always made a point of going out before they came back, so we hardly ever exchanged any words: how could I learn any English? I also had my lunch every day at the Wimpy bar; I used to buy a type of burger in a bun, a kind of early MacDonald's: not very healthy food, I am afraid. Indeed, I put on weight because of that. Later on, I resolved to lose all the weight I had gained, so I went on a starvation diet during the week, but on Saturdays I used to relax the rules and practically binge-eat, which is the worst thing anybody can do, as it is extremely unhealthy. I also borrowed a bike and went on long rides, except that I was rather silly riding like crazy down Boar's Hill, near Oxford, hands-free and at great speed. Completely irresponsible, especially as I was not wearing a crash helmet. I was lucky not to be killed!

Coming back to my au pair experience in North Oxford, I did end up learning a couple of phrases with the family. Once Mrs Gilbert called me from upstairs and said "Anna, have you got the time?" I did not understand, but recognised the word 'time' and thought she meant the Times newspaper! So, I took the newspaper up to her. I knew what she meant the following time she asked me that same question! I also learnt a few words and phrases with the two children, who were actually very sweet and nice to me!

I missed my family too, in spite of the fact that they were the reason why I had to leave home. Furthermore, the skies seemed to be forever grey in this country: I was not used to the darkness we were getting every day and it all added to my depression and discontent.

There was another problem. Mr Gilbert was supposed to pay me £1 a week, a wage of sorts, but he often conveniently 'forgot' to let me have the money. Can you imagine how unhappy I was about that? I needed that money to buy my burger buns at the Wimpy bar every day! I was forced to ask him for the money and absolutely hated having to do that because I found it very demeaning. I started thinking that I could no longer stay there because I was being exploited and I could no longer accept that: I had no respect for such people who seemed to think only about their own gains and showed no empathy towards me and my needs!

Meanwhile, I had met a frequent visitor to the house, a mechanic called Denis, who worked at the Cowley Morris factory and looked after the Gilberts' car- they had met through their political ideologies, as they were all left-wing. Denis soon asked me out and we started a relationship of some sort; he was very reserved and not at all what you would call a romantic! I stopped visiting my Spanish friends and spent more time with Denis's friends. Afterwards he used to drop me off at the top of the road in the early hours of the morning, which was not a clever thing to do, as it wasn't really safe for a lone young woman to be walking along that deserted road at that time of the night. In fact, once someone crept up behind me and hit me with a hard flick of his hand on my lower back. It was really painful. Thankfully it wasn't a knife; the incident left me shaken but unharmed! From that moment I never again allowed Denis to drop me off other than outside the house!

However, we had fun and did mad things together, including joining his communist student friends at parties held in the colleges in Oxford. Often, I had to climb a high wall, as that was the only way to enter after the gates were closed for the night; we laughed a lot, as I had to be pushed up the wall by Denis and all the others.

Through an Austrian girl, who was also working as an au pair for one of the neighbours, I found out that there was a college, Plater College, looking for girls to work there, also on an au pair arrangement. At around Easter, I announced to the family that I would be leaving; Mrs Gilbert was devastated and tried a sob story that she had exams coming up and needed me even more at that stage. Obviously, I ignored all that, as I absolutely loathed my time spent with that family; besides, I had already given them a lot of help with nothing much in return, therefore I did not hesitate to leave when I had the chance to do so.

CHAPTER 6

MY EVENTFUL LIFE IN THE UK

In Plater College, North Hinksey, near Oxford, we were treated well and, after doing a few chores, had a lot of free time. It was a happy period of my life. My English was improving, although I still did not know vocabulary which occasionally would have been essential, such as the word 'fire'. One day, one of the other girls was foolish enough to put a lump of wax in a plastic bowl on the gas cooker in the kitchen in order to melt it before applying it to the parquet floors and then left the room. I was serving lunch to the students in the dining room. When I went into the kitchen to fetch something or other, I saw that the wax had ignited and a big flame was reaching the ceiling; in a panic, I ran back into the dining room and shouted "Quickly, come! There is 'something' in the kitchen!" - I did not know the word 'fire', which was rather unfortunate, as they must have thought I had seen perhaps a little mouse or a bee and did not react at all. It was only after seeing me really agitated that someone went into the kitchen. Then it was mayhem; by then the kitchen was half destroyed! Years later, when I taught languages and used to set vocabulary learning, I always related that story to my students to stress the importance of knowing the correct words when speaking a foreign language.

I have many amusing memories of my time working

in Plater College. Once, for example, I was instructed to prepare custard and stewed plums for the students' pudding - I did not know that the plums were to be served separately from the custard, which would then be poured on top. I thought they should be immersed in the custard, which was terribly watery anyway. They were floating on top of the yellowy concoction, which definitely did not look like custard nor tasted like it! As I was not aware of measurements other than litres and grams and knew nothing about ounces and pounds mentioned in the instructions, I did not use the right amount of powder for the custard! It was a complete fiasco! The poor students had no dessert that day! We laughed about this for ages afterwards.

The end of the summer term arrived; the exams

were over and the students returned home, just leaving the au pair girls there. Only some of the girls were reappointed for the following year, as the number of students at the college was in decline, so they needed fewer staff to work there; understandably they applied 'the last to arrive, the first to leave' principle. They also chose the Staff who could offer the most skills, such as being able to cook. I was the very last girl to be appointed and I was useless at cooking, so I did not have my contract renewed, which meant that I should have left to go back to France after a year from my arrival (end of November) - the chance of getting a renewed visa without a contract was nil.

In August I travelled back to France for about two weeks, but could not wait to get back to England and the carefree life I had here. So back I came, but I was devastated about the prospect of having to leave for good in November. At some point after the summer, Denis declared that he had the solution to the problem: we would get married, so I could not be deported! I suppose he must have thought it was a good way of getting one up on the Establishment. By then it was already October; time was running out, so I accepted his proposition and turned up at the Registry Office on the twenty-second of that month, with just two witnesses - Denis's Oxford University student friends. Nobody else knew anything about the marriage. I became pregnant with my son Max quite quickly, so we were forced to tell Denis's parents about the wedding and the pregnancy; they were actually delighted by the news.

CHAPTER 7

MARRIED AND POOR YET AGAIN

Denis knew that I had been to university, so he made the decision to go back into education, sit some O' and A' Levels and become an Art teacher. Presumably he must have felt rather inferior to me and decided to better himself through studying. I thought that was the right thing to do. He gave up his job as a mechanic and applied for a grant to support us both whilst he studied. The grant was a derisory amount, insufficient to cover our basic needs. Also, Denis would go to the pub with his friends almost every night and would spend much of the money meant to buy food on beer. I was experiencing poverty again!

At first, whilst I was pregnant, we lived in Oxford. When the baby was due, I was admitted to the Maternity Unit at the Churchill Hospital in Oxford. Persecuted by bad luck as usual, the only delivery room was occupied, so I was given a side room and practically left to fend for myself. The story of my life, really! The pain was excruciating, but no one came to help me. Denis was there for a short while, trying to read a newspaper which he had laid out on the bed: he seemed unable to show any empathy towards me! When the pain became unbearable, I gave a mighty kick and knocked the newspaper on the floor. After that, he went home to sleep, he said. So, I was completely on my own until a young student nurse heard my cries and came in. Just as well, as after a very short while my son was born! Afterwards I had to be stitched up: the delivery had been very traumatic, not only mentally, but also physically.

For a while we lived in a rented flat along Iffley Road, not far from an imposing Catholic church. I was brought up as a Catholic, like everyone else in Chieti, although my parents were just following tradition when they baptised us and made sure we also received First Communion. However, as I had only married Denis in the Registry Office, I felt a terrible sense of guilt. I thought my parents would be horrified that mine was not a marriage in the eyes of the Church too. I resolved not to tell them about it; I believe in always telling the truth, but in that instance I did not feel I had a choice and a white lie was fully justified, because I thought they would never forgive me if they knew the facts.

I commissioned a printed invitation to a fictitious wedding at the Catholic church nearby, knowing that no member of my family would ever turn up at such a short notice; in fact, I sent the invitation literally only the week before the imaginary marriage date. The mail to Europe was very slow in those days, so my communication did not get there until ten days after the 'wedding'. That strategy got me out of a sticky situation, as it all went according to plans: nobody turned up of course and when asked for any wedding photographs, I replied that we could not afford a photographer!

However, I thought that at least I should ensure that my son would be baptised as a Catholic, so I went to see the priest at the nearby church. He was not a nice person at all and there was nothing charitable and forgiving about him! When he heard that my marriage to Denis did not include a religious ceremony, he was horrified: he said I should be ashamed of myself for being a sinner! Consequently, if I wanted my son to be baptised, I should ask God for forgiveness and the way to do that was to go from the door of the church to the altar on my knees!! It was quite a long way and the pain was excruciating! I don't know why I agreed to that barbaric form of punishment! I have since regretted it, as my knees must have been damaged by those hard marble floors. Furthermore, why did I have to be 'punished'? I had not committed any crimes! It is unbelievable that a priest could be so cruel and sadistic: it was a form of torture. After that, the Baptism took place, but I lost faith in the Catholic Church and have never set foot in one of their churches since. My second marriage took place in a Baptist church.

When Max was about eight months old, we moved into a council house in Berinsfield, a village situated at about twenty miles from Oxford, but had very little furniture, mostly donated to us by Denis's friends and relatives. We had no fridge, no washing machine and the cooker was old and did not work too well. Life was hard for me, as we only had Denis's grant and, in any case, he never gave me any of that money. In desperation, I had to join my neighbour Marlene in going to one of the local farms to pick peas, with Max in a pushchair. We were paid a pittance according to the number of boxes of peas we had managed to pick; with a child in tow, I never managed more than a few crates for a whole day's work.

Thankfully, after a summer of absolute poverty, in October the evening classes restarted, so I was lucky to be reappointed as a teacher of French and Italian three nights a week. It was hard driving back afterwards, often in very thick fog in the middle of the winter. Denis let me drive his Morris Minor and agreed to stay at home with our son. However, we were poles apart in our attitude to life, values and beliefs, so we did not get on at all; actually, you could say that we were completely incompatible. Also, I was especially unhappy with him when I told him that one of his friends, who started visiting me at the house when he was out, one day approached me from behind and hugged me, whilst I was standing by the sink! I moved away swiftly and told him not to do that again. I was not expecting anything like that to happen, but there must have been signs, which I had failed to spot because of my naivety. Denis's reaction was to laugh about the incident. I was horrified, as I thought he would confront his friend and tell him, in no uncertain terms, that his behaviour was unacceptable; instead, he was amused and I felt unprotected and vulnerable as a result.

As I said, Denis was out on the nights I was not teaching. He was also out on important days such as Christmas and the New Year. He never showed any sympathy for the fact that I had to stay at home with the child and also that we only had the Morris Minor, so, if he used it, I had no means of transport and I could not go out: Berinsfield was out in the sticks. The hardest time was New Year's Eve! It wasn't easy being on my own, when I knew everybody else was celebrating surrounded by family and friends. I was lonely again! And poor! History was repeating itself. So, when Max was eighteen months old, after spending one New Year's Eve crying and singing "We shall overcome one day…" I made the decision to leave and go back to France. In fact, my mother and brother arrived one day to collect my few possessions and took Max and me back to Lucenay.

Denis soon decided to join us in France and worked as a mechanic for about three months, but it was clear that we could not stay there indefinitely, so I let him convince me to give another go at our marriage and I came back to England. As I thought my son was old enough to go to a nursery, I applied to train as a teacher at Westminster College near Oxford. Prior to that, I had applied to go to Oxford University proper. I was accepted thanks to my diploma of Maturita` Classica, my studies at Bari University and my French Diploma, pending the results of an entrance examination I would have had to sit. I concluded that my English was still not good enough for that examination, so I accepted Westminster College's invitation to start a teacher's course there in the coming September instead. It was 1970. My English improved fast - in leaps and bounds - and soon I was achieving high marks in all my assignments (although I was still producing howlers such as 'canning' instead of 'caning' for example).

My relationship with Denis did not improve at all, actually it got worse and we ended up only just tolerating each other. Now that I could fully understand what he was saying, our outlook on life and our principles were even more distant. I started thinking that we should separate; however, it was easier said than done, as I had a child to consider. After qualifying as a teacher, I immediately started teaching at the local middle school. Finally, I was earning good money!

The first thing I did after receiving my first salary was to buy a fridge, a cooker and a washing machine. Unfortunately, I could not pay cash, so I had to go for a hire purchase agreement and pay in instalments. But guess what? I had no right to take a HP contract in my name as I was a married woman! Denis had to sign the agreement, so, even though I paid for those appliances, they were in effect his property. Is that justice? Was a woman just her husband's chattel in 1970s Britain? Clearly that was the case! In fact, when I left him a couple of years later, I could not take those items with me as they legally belonged to him!

CHAPTER 8

A NEW JOB AND A NEW LIFE

At Westminster College I had qualified as a teacher of French, but my ambition was also to teach Italian. One day, as I was looking at the teaching posts advertised in the TES, I spotted an advert for a teacher of Italian with French at The Meadway School in Reading, so I applied, as travelling to Reading would not be a problem: in fact, Denis, who had also qualified as a teacher at the same time as I did, was already teaching at another Reading school and could give me a lift.

I was successful in my interview and got the job. I

started teaching there in September 1973. At first it was a bit of a shock to the system, as I had spent a year teaching at a 'well-to-do' middle school - a real cushy number. Teaching there had been a walk in the park, but the Meadway School was a bit more challenging. However, I soon loved the camaraderie amongst the teachers, which created such a lovely atmosphere in the staffroom. We used to laugh a lot, thanks to the great sense of humour of colleagues such as Adrian Roach and John Sharp, who are still loyal friends of mine alongside John Beasley.

The great majority of the students were such great kids, interspersed with rough diamonds, who, individually, were challenging at times, but deep down great too. I really loved all the years I spent there and I am very proud to have been the longest serving teacher. I am also proud of all the students I had the pleasure of guiding. There are even some famous names amongst them: a very well-known Shakespearian actor and film director, who has been given a Knighthood; a TV presenter; a Commonwealth games medal winner; an actress and many others. Some have become teachers, lawyers etc. There was also a Mayor! So many other amazing pupils, such as Oliver Hunter, Sara and Louise Wild, have grown into fine adults.

I am also proud to have worked as Chief Examiner of GCSE Italian for the Oxford Examination Board for a few years. I loved the challenge of setting all the written papers every year, which I found so rewarding.

In Reading I met my second husband, Steve. It seemed as though fate was trying very hard to get us together: we had literally bumped into each other three times, before we met at a party organised by a Meadway teacher and her flatmate who was Steve's colleague. That was forty-four years ago, in 1975. My marriage to Steve has brought me stability and I have spent forty-three years of our married life looking after our family, getting on with my teaching and finally enjoying a reasonable standard of living.

However, my fear of being poor compelled me to take very short periods of maternity leave after the birth of both my daughters. I regret this, as it put me physically under duress, especially when my daughter Julia contracted whooping cough and needed assistance overnight; this lasted a few months, during which I had to sleep on a makeshift bed in her room and was up several times every night. I still went to work every day in spite of the little sleep I had. I also think it was unfair to my daughters to be sent to a nursery so young, instead of having me looking after them until they started school. If I could go back, I would do things differently.

Thankfully I have not had to battle any more with poverty and solitude! However, I often think about the suffering of those who live in poor countries or in areas ravaged by war and think how lucky I really am! At least I was given the chance of overcoming those difficulties and eventually attained a satisfactory standard of living. My life story demonstrates that certainly nature (innate ability) can prevail even if there is no nurture and that education is key to earning power. In fact, in comparison to the suffering of some poor people in other parts of the world, perhaps my life has not been too bad after all, although I wonder whether the stress and deprivation I have suffered could have been the root cause of the Parkinson's which is ravaging my body! I seem to have drawn the short straw yet again...Truly the story of my life. However, according to an Italian saying 'Dove c'e` vita, c'e` speranza' (Where there is life, there is hope). So, after such an epic journey, I am even more determined not to surrender yet!

APPENDIX

(IMAGES)

The Abruzzo region outlined.

Chieti, 14 miles from Pescara.

The outline of Gran Sasso at dusk.

A section of GRAN SASSO.

PRETORO, a typical Abruzzo village, with Maiella behind.

An aerial view of Chieti.

Local women balancing highly decorated baskets on their heads.

My mother Maria Ciancetta aged 20.

My father Antonio Di Lorenzo aged 23.

The flat on the top floor of the block on the right.

My wonderful paternal grandmother Maria Vincenza D'Anastasio.

My paternal grandfather Domenico Di Lorenzo, a First World War hero.

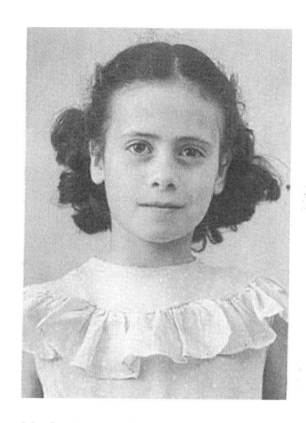

My first ever photo at the age of 11.

My Christmas letter to my parents in 1953.

My American uncle Alfonso with my grandmother and
one of her brothers in Pianella in 1951.

With Niny in Chieti, in 1961.

Niny's beachside villa, mysteriously burnt one night.

With my uncle Domenico in Chieti before I moved to France.

With my classmates from liceo classico on a day trip to the Abruzzi mountains. I am the first from the right standing.

Antoine, the French lad I met at the age of 16.

Photo taken in Bari whilst at university there.

With the party of French youngsters I accompanied on a tour of Italy in 1966.

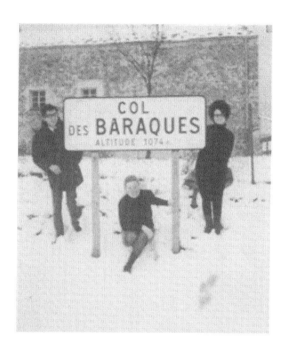

With the Japanese lad who wanted to marry me and another friend from the French course at Lyon University.

Shortly after my arrival in the UK in 1966, with a

'beehive' hairstyle.

Mr Gilbert with David and Michelle.

My first husband Denis McEvoy.

My return to Lyon with Max.

With my second husband Stephen Greaves.

My first photo as a teacher at the Meadway School, Reading, with the rest of the Staff. I am the fourth from the left, second row from the back.

48606678R00101

Printed in Poland
by Amazon Fulfillment
Poland Sp. z o.o., Wrocław